Copyright © 2025 Peter Griffiths T
based on the THIRD EDITION co]
author passed away in 1950, over
since that year, as such, the THIRD EDITION is in the
public domain.

The changes, to aid the reader, in this digital version are copyrighted by Peter Griffiths 2024.

Unless otherwise stated, scripture quotations are from The ESV® Bible (The Holy Bible, English Standard Version®), © 2001 by Crossway, a publishing ministry of Good News Publishers. Scripture taken from the New King James Version®. Copyright © 1982 by Thomas Nelson. Used by permission. All rights reserved.

# The Modern Tongues Movement

Examined And Judged In The Light Of The Scripture And In The Light Of Its Fruit

# By Louis S. Bauman, D. D.
(1875 – 1950)

In a day when so many, who solemnly profess to be children of God, are unconsciously becoming the victims of demonic influences, no faithful shepherd can refuse to solemnly warn the flock. Probably the most widely spread of all Satanic phenomena today is the demonic imitation of the apostolic gift of tongues. It is extremely common in the realms of Spiritism, Islamism and Mormonism. It is seen in witchcraft, in pagan oracles, in heathen temples and prophethoods, and all other neurotic manias and frenzies. It appeared very early in the history of the Christian church in that demonic movement known as Montanism. The first miracle that Satan ever wrought was to cause the Serpent to speak in a tongue. (Genesis 3:1). It would appear he is still working his original miracle.

It may be pointed out that some exceedingly fine people are exercising the gift of tongues in our day. That matters not, for the "good man" argument never proves anything. The Apostle Paul long ago warned us that there would be **"false apostles, deceitful workmen, disguising themselves as apostles of Christ. And no wonder, for even Satan disguises himself as an angel of light. So it is no surprise if his servants, also, disguise themselves as servants of righteousness"** (II Cor. 11:13-15). Our Lord made an exceedingly solemn statement when He said: **"On that day many will say to me, 'Lord, Lord, did we not prophesy in your name, and cast out demons in your name, and do many mighty works in your name?' 23 And then will I declare to them, 'I never knew you; depart from me, you workers of lawlessness.'"** (Matt. 7:22-23). No matter how great the culture, refinement or seeming virtues of the "angels of light" who may come to us, we must take our stand and cry: **"To the law and to the testimony! If they speak not according to this word, it is because there is no light in them"** (Isaiah 8:20 KJV).

Men and women, famed for apparent extreme piety, have been among the most notable victims of Satan in the Tongues Movement, falling away into deepest sin and awful heresies. Of some of such we shall speak later. Living, as we are, in the last days, we need constantly to bear in mind the solemn warning of the Master: **"Then if anyone says to you, 'Look, here is the Christ!' or 'There he is!' do not believe it. For false christs and false prophets will arise and perform great signs and wonders, so as to lead astray, if possible, even the elect."** (Matt. 24:23-26).

In the discussion of this subject, there is another peril of which we are not unmindful. In the apostolic church there was a genuine gift of the Spirit, known as speaking in tongues. To attribute to Satan or to demons any genuine work of the Holy Ghost is a matter of gravest peril. (Mark 3:28-30). It therefore behooves us, before condemning an experience as being of Satan, to heed the solemn admonition of the Word of God and "test the spirits to see whether they are from God" (I John 4:1). By all means, never condemn until you have tested the spirits by the Word of God. Likewise, by all means never receive until you have tested the spirits by the Word of God.

It appears that there were two kinds of tongues that emanated from the Holy Spirit in the days of the apostles. **First**, the tongue of a known language, as on the day of Pentecost.

**Secondly,** the tongue of an "unknown" language, as set forth in the 14th chapter of I Corinthians. (It is to be noted that the word "unknown" is supplied by the translators. However, the context clearly shows that it is rightly supplied.) We need to consider carefully the outstanding chapter of all Scripture on this subject, namely, I Corinthians 14. A careful perusal of this chapter sets forth the following facts:

## 1. The True Gift Of Tongues Was The Least Of The Holy Spirit's Gifts.

Turning to Chapters 12 and 13, which should be considered carefully in connection with the study of Chapter 14, we note the following facts.

**First -** In two listings of the gifts of the Spirit (I Cor. 12:1-11 and 28-30), the gift of tongues, with its companion gift of interpretation, is placed last.

**Second -** The Apostle Paul counts love the greatest of all gifts; and, declares that, **"If I speak in the tongues of men and of angels, but have not love, I am a noisy gong or a clanging cymbal."** (I Cor. 13:1). After setting forth those two facts, the great Apostle then plunges into his dissertation on the unknown tongue:

> **"Pursue love, and earnestly desire the spiritual gifts, especially that you may prophesy. For one who speaks in a tongue speaks not to men but to God; for no one understands him, but he utters mysteries in the Spirit. On the other hand, the one who prophesies speaks to people for their**

upbuilding and encouragement and consolation. The one who speaks in a tongue builds up himself, but the one who prophesies builds up the church. Now I want you all to speak in tongues, but even more to prophesy. The one who prophesies is greater than the one who speaks in tongues, unless someone interprets, so that the church may be built up.

Now, brothers, if I come to you speaking in tongues, how will I benefit you unless I bring you some revelation or knowledge or prophecy or teaching? If even lifeless instruments, such as the flute or the harp, do not give distinct notes, how will anyone know what is played? And if the bugle gives an indistinct sound, who will get ready for battle? So with yourselves, if with your tongue you utter speech that is not intelligible, how will anyone know what is said? For you will be speaking into the air. There are doubtless many different languages in the world, and none is without meaning, but if I do not know the meaning of the language, I will be a foreigner to the speaker and the speaker a foreigner to me. So with yourselves, since you are eager for manifestations of the Spirit, strive to excel in building up the church.

Therefore, one who speaks in a tongue should pray that he may interpret. For if I pray in a tongue, my spirit prays but my mind is unfruitful. What am I to do? I will pray with my spirit, but I will pray with my mind also; I will sing praise with my spirit, but I will sing with my mind also. Otherwise, if you give thanks with your spirit, how can anyone in the position of an outsider say "Amen" to your thanksgiving when he does not know what you are saying? For you may be giving thanks well enough, but the other person is not being built up. I thank God that I speak in tongues more than all of you. Nevertheless, in church I would rather speak five words with my mind in order to instruct others, than ten thousand words in a tongue." (I Cor. 14:1-19).

It is impossible to read these words without realising the fact that though there was a genuine gift of tongues, yet it was the least of all gifts and far, far below the gift of prophesying: and let us bear in mind that the word "Prophesy," as used by the Apostle, literally means "to publicly expound," and is so translated in Young's Concordance. In his letter to the Ephesians, the Apostle Paul again lists the gifts of the Spirit. (4:11). Here there is not even mention made of the gift of tongues, upon which some place such great stress today.

We solemnly charge the modern "tongues" people with making the least of all the spiritual gifts the most emphasized doctrine of the whole Movement. What Paul places at the bottom of the list, they place at the top. Though the Apostle makes the gift of prophecy (i.e., "Rightly dividing the Word of Truth") the infinitely greater gift, yet the modern Tongues proponents set themselves forth as competent judges and critics of the man who has this gift and would belittle his ministry unless he also speaks in tongues. It would seem to us that those who possess the lesser gift might be a bit humbler in the presence of those who possess the greater. But ARE they?

They even go further, and set their babbling "experiences" above the Word of God itself. We know of authentic instances where people who talked in tongues claimed that their revelations were sufficient revelations of the will of God, and that therefore they had no further use for the Bible itself! Why should they need the Bible when God is talking with them directly? We can only say that it is fearfully dangerous business, this business of turning from the written Word, handed down to us by Christ and His apostles; and, turning to the utterances of uncertain spirits, not even tested by the Word.

Little is the wonder that we find in the modern Tongues Movement, a Mr. J. I. MacDonald, in England, writing a tract defending speaking in tongues, and therein comes out boldly in defense of one of the earliest Tongues proponents, Montanus. But, listen! Montanus, who had originally been a priest of Cybele, said: "I am the Father, the Word, and the Paraclete: I am the Lord God Omnipotent who have descended into man!" Awful are the illusions that overtake men who forget that the revelation of the Lord God of the heavens for this dispensation is full, complete, and final, in the written Word of God, The Bible.

How significant it is that the Apostle should draw to a close his exhortation on the subject of tongues with the admonition: "So, my brothers, earnestly desire to prophesy, and do not forbid speaking in tongues." (I Cor. 14:39). Here is a great urge to seek the great gift of expounding the Word;

but when it comes to tongues, instead of there being an urge to seek it, he simply admonishes them to "forbid not to speak with tongues." How could it be otherwise when "five words with my mind in order to instruct others" are of far greater value "than ten thousand in a tongue"?

Once again, we charge the Tongues Movement with making the gift of tongues the supreme evidence for "the baptism of the Holy Ghost," whereas it must be apparent to every candid mind that **the supreme test for the infilling of the Holy Ghost is to be found in "fruit of the Spirit"**; and "the fruit of the Spirit is love, joy, peace, patience, kindness, goodness, faithfulness, gentleness, self-control" (Gal. 5:22-23).

## 2. The True Gift Of Tongues Was For "A Sign."

**"Thus, tongues are a sign"** (v. 22). This statement of the Apostle is backed by the Master Himself: **"And these signs will accompany those who believe: in my name they will cast out demons; they will speak in new tongues;"** etc. (Mark 16:17).

It needs to be noted that signs are for the Jews rather than for Gentiles: "For Jews demand signs and Greeks seek wisdom" (I Cor. 1:22). Over and over, the Jews sought for signs. "Teacher, we wish to see a sign from you." But he answered them, "An evil and adulterous generation seeks for a sign" (Matt. 12:38-39). Again: "Then what sign do you do, that we may see and believe you"? (John 6:30). (See also Matt. 16:1-4 and John 2:18). As a matter of fact, this love for signs is to be, at last, Israel's sad undoing. It actually will cause the Jewish people some of these days to receive the Antichrist as their Messiah; and, sad, sad will be their awakening! Let us leave signs to the Jews, if they wish them. It is for the Church of the Living God to "walk by faith, not by sight." (II Cor. 5:7).

## 3. The True Gift Of Tongues Was For The Purpose Of Confirming The Word

Note the record of Mark (16:15-20): ""Go into all the world and proclaim the gospel to the whole creation... And these signs will accompany those who believe: in my name they will cast out demons; they will speak in new tongues; they will pick up serpents with their hands; and if they drink any deadly poison, it will not hurt them; they will lay their hands on the sick, and they will recover."... And they went out and preached everywhere, while the Lord worked with them and confirmed the message by accompanying signs."

Such confirmation by divine manifestations was a necessary adjunct to their preaching, since at that time the apostles had no other confirmation for their message. The Gospel was first offered to the Jew. When the first disciples approached the Jews with the message of the new covenant, we readily can see that the Jews would challenge their authority for preaching against a continuance of the ceremonies and rites of Moses. If anyone challenges our message today, we appeal to the inspired message of the New Testament; but, the first disciples (the New Testament being yet unwritten) were compelled to depend upon the Holy Spirit backing their appeals by manifestations of the supernatural, seen in the miracles that accompanied their message. On the day of Pentecost, speaking in tongues confirmed the message of Peter and convinced the Jews mightily (Acts 2:3-13). When Peter carried the message to the Gentiles, both Jews and Gentiles were convinced mightily through the supernatural sign (Acts 10:44-48). Once again, when Paul "came to Ephesus. There he found some disciples. And he said to them, "Did you receive the Holy Spirit when you believed?" And they said, "No, we have not even heard that there is a Holy Spirit."" (Acts 19:1-2). Thereupon, these disciples were given the same confirming sign that the Apostles themselves had received on the day of Pentecost.

The Apostle emphatically stated, "as for tongues, they will cease" (I Cor. 13:8). We can readily believe that the time they were to cease was the time when the inspired Apostles laid down their pens, having completed the New Testament the final and authoritative revelation of God for our age. Almost the last stroke of a pen in a hand moved by the Holy Spirit (II Pet. 1:21) was to solemnly warn: "if anyone adds to them, God will add to him the plagues described in this book" (Rev. 22:18). In the light of this warning, is it reasonable to suppose that additions to the revelation of God were thereafter in order through tongues or otherwise? It is significant that when Paul wrote his epistle to the Corinthians, and placed so little stress upon the gift of tongues, it was twenty-five years after Pentecost and the pen of his inspiration was busily at work. Again, it is significant to note that when Dives asked Abraham for "a sign," the sign was refused him for one simple reason: **"They have Moses** and the prophets. Let them hear them" And when he insisted that if "**someone goes to them from the dead, they will repent.**" Abraham promptly replied: "**If they do not hear Moses and the Prophets, neither will they be convinced if someone should rise from the dead.**" (See Luke 16:19-31). And, if today, men, regenerate or unregenerate, reject the inspired Word of God, they need expect no signs from heaven. Signs usher in dispensations, at which time signs have their place of usefulness. Signs ushered in the Church Age; after the Church is caught away to meet her Lord in the air, signs will usher in the Millennial Age. But, in each case, remember, the signs serve the Jews.

## 4. The True Gift Of Tongues Can Be Counterfeited By Satanic Spirits, And Was Thus Counterfeited In The Apostolic Church.

Consider the confusion wrought in the church at Corinth: "If, therefore, the whole church comes together and all speak in tongues, and outsiders or unbelievers enter, will they not say that you are out of your minds? ... What then, brothers? When you come together, each one has a hymn, a lesson, a revelation, a tongue, or an interpretation... For God is not a God of confusion but of peace." (I Cor. 14:23-33).

It is quite evident from the entire chapter that this "gift of tongues" was working untold confusion in the Corinthian Church. Now then, **"God is not a God of confusion"** (v. 33). If God was not the author of the tongue-confusion in the Church at Corinth, **who was the author?**

As a matter of fact, confusion is the one thing that characterizes the modern tongues meetings everywhere. Bedlam might be a better word. This fact is so well known that it admits of no argument. Right here in Southern California we have personal knowledge that the police have been called at times to quiet neighborhoods which have been disturbed by their meetings. The true gift of tongues never wrought confusion. The speaking in tongues on the day of Pentecost was a decent and orderly procedure, else how could it have been asked, "And how is it that we hear, each of us in his own native language"? (Acts 2:8). It is true that "others, mocking said, they are filled with new wine" (Acts 2:13). Any fair-minded person will candidly admit that if you should hear members of your own family, never having known the Chinese language, for instance, suddenly burst forth speaking that language—a language wholly unknown to you—it would seem like the speech of a drunken man, even though it should be spoken decently and in order. The confusion of a modern "tongues meeting" cannot be set in the Biblical picture of Pentecost.

Contrast the difference: At a great Pentecost meeting in San Jose, where as many as ten thousand people attended, a certain preacher was "seeking the baptism," when a prominent woman worker approached him, and, chucking him under the chin, said, "Now, just imagine you are a baby and begin to babble!" Imagine Peter, on the day of Pentecost, going around chucking the Jews under their chins, saying, "Now, just imagine you are babies, and begin to babble"!

We have in our possession a pamphlet by Sir Robert Anderson, K. C. B., LL. D., published in London, on the subject, "Spirit Manifestations and The Gift of Tongues," in which he quoted the personal experience of one of the leaders of the Tongues Movement in India. This experience is taken from a pamphlet issued by the leader himself. We quote in part:

"How good God is! Some twelve years ago, I began to long for Pentecost as described in the Bible, and all these years I have been praying for that baptism. Now that I am actually speaking in tongues and living in the daily experience of the presence of the Holy Ghost, it is all so wonderful that it is more like a dream than reality... For the first time, I knelt at the altar on Sunday afternoon, March 17, and the power began to seize me, and I laughed all through the following Communion service. In the evening about 11pm, I knelt with a few of the friends praying for me (Elder "S." placed his hands on my head for a short time, several times during the afternoon and evening). After some little waiting, I began to laugh, or rather my body was used to laugh with increasing power until I was flat on my back, laughing at the top of my voice for over half an hour. On arising, I found that I was drunk on the new wine (Ephesians 5:18), acting just like a drunken man in many ways, and full of joy. On kneeling to meet the Lord again, I was gradually seized with an irresistible power of beseechings and groanings that could not be uttered... Again kneeling, my eyes grew dark, and I was rolled over on to the floor, lying there some time nearly unconscious.[1] Then coming to, and kneeling, I felt my jaws

---

[1] A striking similarity to the work of the demon in the days of Christ: And he (the demon possessed) fell on the ground and rolled about, foaming at the mouth (Mark 9:20).

and mouth being worked by a strange force. In a few seconds some baby gibberish was uttered, then a few words in Chinese that I understood, and then several sentences in a strange tongue. This turned into singing, and I did not speak again in tongues until Wednesday, three days later. After two hours it was done and about 1am. began the most wonderful part of my life thus far. Oh, the great, unspeakable glory of being able to actually praise the God and Saviour of men in the spirit! The next two nights, I was awakened up early in the morning, and given an hour's music lesson, being taught how to yield my throat so as to sing. This was done in such a muffled manner that it disturbed no one in the crowded apartment house where I was sleeping."

Now, imagine the Holy Spirit being engaged in teaching music in a manner like that! However, if this was truly an experience of the Holy Spirit, it would seem that the same spirit ought to put a muffler on the throats of a lot of other people in the Tongues Movement, who are prone to disturb the peace of whole neighborhoods at unseemly hours of the night!

And, sometimes stranger sounds than mere "baby gibberish" leap forth from the lips of those who have surrendered their lips to any spirit-force that may wish to move them. Sometimes, the utterances seem to come forth from the pit itself. Some of these strange noises give direct evidence of being produced by the Serpent. One, who was in touch with Irvingism, that famous "tongues movement," testified: "To stand by her (a prophetess) was like being near a nest of serpents, as the hissing she made while under the paroxysms exactly resembled those serpents."

Moreover, when we hear the babbling, the "baby gibberish," and the uncanny hissings in connection with the modern Tongues Movement, nearly always it is connected with uncanny twistings or convulsions of the face or body or both, so unlike any work of the Holy Ghost, though we do read of such contortions resulting from demon possession.

## 5. The True Gift Of Speaking In An Unknown Tongue Was A Means Of Private Edification, And Was To Be Exercised But Little, If At All, In Public.

In a day when Christians were as yet without the New Testament Scriptures, we can imagine that there would be some edification through revelation from the Spirit of God in this manner. Today a devout search of that which God has "in these last days he has spoken to us by his Son" (Heb. 1:2) is of more certain edification. Again, let the Apostle speak:

> "For one who speaks in a tongue speaks not to men but to God; for no one understands him, but he utters mysteries in the Spirit. On the other hand, the one who prophesies speaks to people for their upbuilding and encouragement and consolation. The one who speaks in a tongue builds up himself, but the one who prophesies builds up the church… For you may be giving thanks well enough, but the other person is not being built up. I thank God that I speak in tongues more than all of you. Nevertheless, in church I would rather speak five words with my mind in order to instruct others, than ten thousand words in a

tongue… But if there is no one to interpret, let each of them keep silent in church and speak to himself and to God." (I Cor 14:2-4, 17-19, 28).

The Apostle Paul talked **"more than all of you"**; and yet, where have we any record that he ever exercised the gift in public? As it was, even in private, he seemed to take no special pride in it. Moreover, it is worthy of note that, while we have sixty-six books within our Bible, yet nowhere have we the slightest indication that a single line of the whole, came through the tongues method of divine revelation! **Why?** Is it possible that it was fraught with too much uncertainty?

## 6. The True Gift Of Tongues Was Not To Be Exercised In Public, Except Some One With The Gift of Interpretation Was Present.

"Now, brothers, if I come to you speaking in tongues, how will I benefit you unless I bring you some revelation or knowledge or prophecy or teaching? If even lifeless instruments, such as the flute or the harp, do not give distinct notes, how will anyone know what is played? And if the bugle gives an indistinct sound, who will get ready for battle? So with yourselves, if with your tongue you utter speech that is not intelligible, how will anyone know what is said? For you will be speaking into the air."(1 Cor 14:6-9) (It must candidly be admitted that the Apostle Paul has aptly described the great mass of tongues speakers in these last days, they **"SPEAK INTO**

**THE AIR.**") "What then, brothers? When you come together, each one has a hymn, a lesson, a revelation, a tongue, or an interpretation. Let all things be done for building up. If any speak in a tongue, let there be only two or at most three, and each in turn, and let someone interpret. But if there is no one to interpret, let each of them keep silent in church and speak to himself and to God." (I Cor 14: 26-29)

Here we have directions that are ignored almost completely by the modern Tongues Movement. Assuredly the Holy Spirit would not ignore His own directions. We fear the working of other spirits—spirits that are not of God.

Some years ago, in Whittier, California, a man arose in an audience to which we were preaching, and began to speak in tongues. Immediately, we asked if there was an interpreter present. Finding none present, we commanded him with some emphasis to "Sit down and keep quiet"! We had the Scriptural right to so demand and to so command. He sat down.

## 7. The True Gift Of Tongues Was Under The Speaker's Control.

We repeat: "If any man speak in an unknown tongue, let it be by two, or at the most by three, and that by course; and let one interpret. But if there be no interpreter, let him keep silence in the church; and let him speak to himself, and to God." (I Cor. 14:27-28). Now, we are compelled to admit that no one speaking in tongues could possibly follow these instructions, unless he should have the power of self-control.

A talented medical missionary to China, a graduate physician, who, after being set free from the mysterious power of this Tongues Movement, became a member of the Church of which the writer is pastor, related her experience through The Sunday School Times (Feb. 19, 1927). The place of her experience was in the city where the modern Tongues Movement in America originated, that hotbed for every false doctrine on the face of the earth, Los Angeles. Quoting directly from her remarkable article, we read:

> "I went to these same two friends who took me first to a large meeting held by an evangelist of their persuasion. I was asked if I would not like to 'tarry' and see if the blessing would be given there. I tarried. One of the men associated with the evangelist dealt with me. He was a coarse, loud-voiced man, who, as I recall, laid hands on me and prayed. He then said to me, 'Now, sister, you are to take this verse, Psalms 68:4, where it says "Extol Him that rideth upon the heavens by His name JAH," and repeat the name JAH, JAH, and the first thing you know, you will be off in tongues'! I felt this to be excessively repulsive, but thought I must see it through and that this was all a part of the necessary humbling process, so I repeated the name JAH like a parrot, but all to no avail. The rest of it did not come as stated by the gentleman. May the Lord forgive me for taking His name in vain, as I now consider that farcical thing to be! Failing there, these two friends encouraged me and took me to the same negress who had given assistance to my sister. After a time of waiting, she

took me in hand, talking to me about myself, saying that I was Pharisaical, self-righteous, proud, and that I must confess my sins and come to the Lord and be saved. I dropped on my knees beside a bench, feeling very miserable. She spoke into my ear a prayer which I said after her like a child. Then she seemed to be rebuking someone, speaking loudly and ending with, 'Loose her and let her go'! and I spoke in tongues. This was on January 27, 1918. A characteristic of this experience, as physically manifested, is the involuntary shaking of the lower jaw which is beyond one's control, and produces babbling. This has been very difficult to overcome. The tendency appears every once in a while, but it is not of the Holy Spirit, as I have proved through sad experience. There was no interpretation of what I had uttered that night, although I spoke to one of the workers nearby, asking if it was not customary to have that given. She did not consider it important. The important thing was that I had been 'baptized with the Holy Ghost.' So, I arose from my knees, somewhat puzzled and a trifle in doubt... She appears to me now like a spiritualist medium gambling with the Word of God. Satan had created 'a mental impression' in me and then verified it 'with a sensation,' for, as I left that house, I was elated, filled with an exhilaration which deceived me into thinking that it was the joy of the Holy Ghost. But was there a little prick of conscience in the background, a latent feeling that all was not right?"

(We are quoting rather fully from this "experience" inasmuch as the victim of it, together with her husband, verified it in their personal conversation with the writer.)

**How utterly contrary all this is to the instruction of the Holy Ghost,**—"The involuntary shaking of the lower jaw, WHICH IS BEYOND ONE'S CONTROL AND PRODUCES BABBLING." The whole teaching of these Tongue speakers is that if you want to get "the gift," you must throw yourself completely out of control. "Give over"! "Let go"! "Give over the control of your personality"! "Lose self-control and pass out of the condition of consciousness"! "You cannot get through until your own personality is yielded to the control of another"! When any human being becomes thus utterly will-less, yielding himself to any spirit seeking control.—What an opportunity for disembodied spirits, known as demons, to find the habitation which they everlastingly seek! Can you wonder at the immoralities that are making the Tongues Movement notorious?

And, how utterly unscriptural is this whole teaching that you must "throw yourself out of control," "give over control," or "lose self-control," in order to possess the gift of the Holy Ghost, and receive the sign of the gift! This, of itself, would seem to stamp the whole procedure as of Satan; for, it is written: "But the fruit of the Spirit is... SELF CONTROL" (Gal. 5:22, 23). The emissaries of Satan ask for no better opportunity than that furnished them by passivity of mind and will. The non-use of a man's will runs before the abject slavery to the devil and all his hosts!

# 8. The True Gift Of Tongues Was Not A Gift bestowed By The Holy Spirit Upon Women.

It was a pen that was moved by the Holy Ghost which wrote:

> "As in all the churches of the saints, the women should keep silent in the churches. For they are not permitted to speak, but should be in submission, as the Law also says. If there is anything they desire to learn, let them ask their husbands at home. For it is shameful for a woman to speak in church."
> (I Cor 14: 33-35)

Be careful to note that the admonition against women speaking in the Church refers to speaking in tongues. The entire 14th chapter of I Corinthians deals with the subject of tongues, and tongues only. Verses 27 to 33 give very definite instructions to men speaking in tongues. Verses 34 to 37 then deal with the subject of women exercising the gift. This passage, **"Let your women keep silence in the churches,"** has to do with revelation direct from God, and has nothing to do with women teaching or preaching what is already revealed. To teach what God has duly revealed is woman's blessed privilege. But it has pleased God, for reasons best known to Himself, to reveal His messages to the world through men. The thought in verse 35 is that if women wish to "learn" anything by way of direct revelation from God, "let them ask their husbands at home," i.e., receive their revelations through their proper heads, their husbands. Now, note the force of Verse 36. It is evident that there were women in the Corinthian Church who stood ready to take issue with the great Apostle of God to the Gentiles. Paul dismisses them with the single exclamation: "Or was it from you that the word of God came? Or are you the only ones it has reached?" That is, "If you ladies at Corinth wish to take issue with me, let me ask you one question: What book in all the inspired Word of God ever came as a revelation through a woman? The Word of God came not from you. It came unto you only. Therein rejoice"!

Some contend that Paul's declaration as to women keeping silence in the churches applied only to the women of the Corinthian Church. Such exposition easily can make shipwreck of Scripture. Are we to take the position that Paul's instructions to these Corinthians with regard to the Holy Communion (I Cor. 11:17-34) are instructions for the Church at Corinth only? Are we to take the position that his instructions with regard to the relations between husband and wife (I Cor. 7) are instructions for the Church at Corinth only? Are we to take the position that his instructions with regard to the discipline of members of the Church guilty of immorality (I Cor. 5) are instructions to the Church at Corinth only? And, are we to treat all other passages of all other letters. written by Paul to the various Churches, in the same manner? If so, and we also give over to the Jews (as some would have us do) the Gospels of Matthew, Mark, Luke and John, and even the Acts—what is left to instruct the rest of us in this Twentieth Century? What nonsense!

We know that it is contended by some sincere souls that women spoke in tongues on the day of Pentecost. However, in the lack of positive proof of that assertion, we must contend that the well-known rule must stand: **"The sum total of Scripture on any subject is the truth of that**

**subject."** Inasmuch as the Holy Spirit explicitly forbids women to attempt to become the spokesmen of revelations coming direct from God, we must take the position that in this matter, no woman spoke on the day of Pentecost. Otherwise, you set the Scripture against itself. The fact that there were present, "together with the women and Mary the mother of Jesus, and his brothers." (Acts 1:14), on the day of Pentecost, does not prove, of necessity, that these women spoke in tongues. A close study of the record of Pentecost in Acts 1 and 2, presents a strong argument against the idea that any divine revelations were spoken through women on that day. The accusation hurled against the disciples by the mockers in the crowd was, "they are filled with new wine" (Acts 2:13). In his defense against this accusation, the Apostle Paul declared that that which was happening was a fulfillment of "what was uttered through the prophet Joel: "'And in the last days it shall be, God declares, that I will pour out my Spirit on all flesh, and your sons and your daughters shall prophesy, and your young men shall see visions, and your old men shall dream dreams; even on my male servants and female servants in those days I will pour out my Spirit, and they shall prophesy." (Acts 2:16-18). Note carefully that when it came to seeing "visions" or to dreaming "dreams," it was distinctly the business of men. Divine revelations were given through visions and dreams. But, when it came to prophesying, that is, expounding the revelations given through men, it was the privilege of "daughters" as well as "sons," and of "male servants" as well as "female servants."

Paul was quite content as a guest in the home of Philip the evangelist,—"He had four unmarried daughters, who prophesied" (Acts 21:9). He had no rebuke for Priscilla, who, with her husband, took the mighty Apollos, "and explained to him the way of God more accurately." (Acts 18:26).

## 9. The True Gift Of Speaking In Tongues Will Never Be Exercised By Anyone Who Is Antagonistic To The Word Of God As Spoken By Christ And His Apostles, Especially The Apostle Paul.

Weigh the statement, "If anyone thinks that he is a prophet, or spiritual, he should acknowledge that the things I am writing to you are a command of the Lord." (I Cor 14:37). Unless the Apostle Paul was a prophet wholly uninspired of God, antagonism to his teaching, especially as it would relate to this gift of tongues, marks a man as being neither "a prophet or spiritual." At this point it is well to weigh the Apostle's statement in his great Epistle to the Galatians (1:8, 9): "But even if we or an angel from heaven should preach to you a gospel contrary to the one we preached to you, let him be accursed." "Paul was serenely confident that he had received his gospel, not of man, but directly from the Lord Jesus Christ, and in the "we" he includes himself!

# Some Common Errors Of The Tongues Movement

At this point, we think it fitting that we should discuss some of the common errors of the Tongues Movement.

1. The error of making the great prophecy of the day of Pentecost a prophecy for a continuing fulfillment. It is true that because of the Jews' rejection of Christ as their king, the prophecy had only a partial fulfillment on the day of Pentecost: and, that the complete fulfillment will be toward the close of the Great Tribulation (Rev. 7), when assuredly there will be a great deliverance in Mount Zion and in Jerusalem (Joel 2:32). "For behold, in those days and at that time, when I restore the fortunes of Judah and Jerusalem, I will gather all the nations and bring them down to the Valley of Jehoshaphat." (Joel 3:1-2). But, the teaching that "Pentecost" is an experience which God's children may expect today, is a gross error. Pentecost was an experience through which the Jews were to pass at a most definitely fixed time. The very word "Pentecost" means "fiftieth." Forty days after the resurrection, Christ ascended into the heavens. Fifty days ("the Fiftieth Day") after the resurrection, the Holy Spirit came from above to abide with the Church during this dispensation. The laws definitely fixed the day:

> "In the first month, on the fourteenth day of the month at twilight, is the Lord's Passover... it is a statute forever throughout your generations in all your dwellings. You shall count seven full weeks from the day after the Sabbath, from the day that you

brought the sheaf of the wave offering. You shall count fifty days to the day after the seventh Sabbath." (Lev. 23:5, 14-16).

Comment is scarcely necessary. God Himself fixed the day of Pentecost definitely,—"fifty days" after the resurrection of Christ. Therefore, it was written by Luke (Acts 2:1): "When the day of Pentecost arrived." On that day, the Holy Spirit, working mightily upon Israel, gathered the first fruits unto the Lord. Precious experiences similar to some. of the experiences of Pentecost, men have enjoyed and still may enjoy; but, to speak of such an experience as "a Pentecost," is not in harmony with the revealed Word of God.

2. Another grave error is the teaching that we should tarry or wait for our "Pentecost." Christ never commanded His apostles to wait for any Pentecost. His command to them was, "tarry in the city of Jerusalem until you are endued with power from on high" (Luke 24:49 NKJV). They were not to tarry FOR, but to tarry "UNTIL." Their tarrying had nothing to do with the bringing about of Pentecost. We might tarry at a station until the train comes, but our tarrying does not bring the train.

3. Another error is the teaching that those who are "baptized" by the Holy Ghost will always speak in tongues, their so speaking being the evidence of their "baptism." More unscriptural teaching than this, one can scarcely imagine. Listen carefully to the voice of the Holy Ghost Himself, speaking through the greatest of all the Apostles:

"Now concerning spiritual gifts, brothers, I do not want you to be uninformed... Now there are varieties of gifts, but the same Spirit; and there are varieties of service, but the same Lord; and there are varieties of activities, but it is the same God who empowers them all in everyone. To each is given the manifestation of the Spirit for the common good. For to one is given through the Spirit the utterance of wisdom, and to another the utterance of knowledge according to the same Spirit, to another faith by the same Spirit, to another gifts of healing by the one Spirit, to another the working of miracles, to another prophecy, to another the ability to distinguish between spirits, to another various kinds of tongues, to another the interpretation of tongues. All these are empowered by one and the same Spirit, who apportions to each one individually as he wills." (I Cor. 12:1, 4-11).

Assuredly, ALL these gifts are not for ALL the saints, for among the saints the Holy Spirit "apportions to each one individually as He wills." The man who has the gift of healing, or the man who has the gift of miracles, or the man who has the gift of prophecy,—is it thinkable that the "brethren" who possess these great gifts are without that precious experience known as "the baptism of the Holy Ghost," while the man who exercises the lesser gift and talks in tongues, possesses "the baptism"? (Personally the writer does not like the expression, "the baptism of the Holy Ghost," as touching the experience of Christians today. We prefer to use the expression of the Apostle Paul in writing to the Ephesians (5:18),—"Be filled with the Spirit.") Honestly, are we to believe that such mighty men of God as Wycliffe, Luther, Knox, Finney, Muller, Moody and Chapman, were never "baptized" with the Holy Ghost because they talked not in tongues? Are we to believe that scores and scores of our mighty men and women of God on foreign fields, many of whom laid down their lives for the faith, never knew the "baptism" of the Holy Ghost, while a lot of insignificant people who have done little or nothing for the Lord, and who, in idle curiosity, have made their chief business the seeking for some peculiar experience, have been so "baptized"? Perish the thought! That the Pentecostal people do so teach can be proven over and over again from the printed utterances of their leaders. The official book of the whole Pentecostal Movement,—"The Broadening Presence,"—is one authority. We read:

**"The sign of the coming of the Holy Spirit at Pentecost was tongues. Therefore, all who receive the Spirit must have this sign. People receiving the baptism with the Holy Ghost will always speak in other tongues, but they may not retain the gift."**

Mrs. Aimee Semple McPherson, in a tract entitled, "Divine Healing," now in the possession of the writer, says: "There is not one passage in Scripture to bear out the assertion that the days of miraculously answered prayer were ever to pass away. Here are some of Christ's instructions that have never been recalled:

**'As ye go, preach, saying, The kingdom of heaven is at hand. Heal the sick, cleanse the lepers, cast out devils; freely ye have received, freely give.'** (Matt. 10:7, 8)!"

Note carefully that in "Christ's instructions that have never been recalled," Mrs. McPherson very conveniently omits one instruction of great importance, i.e., to "raise the dead." One might be kind enough to believe that this omission was accidental on her part, or a typographical error. But, what are we to believe when she turns to Mark (16:17, 18) for more of "Christ's instructions that have never been recalled," and quotes thus:

**"And these signs shall follow them that believe! In My name they shall cast out devils; they shall speak with new tongues; they shall lay hands on the sick, and they shall recover,'"**

Now, is it not rather strange that, among **"Christ's instructions that have never been recalled,"** Mrs. McPherson should have accidentally (?) omitted the following instructions: **"They shall take up serpents; and if they drink any deadly thing, it shall not hurt them"**? We are inclined to believe that we can best discern the real reason for the omissions made in these two passages from the next statement in her tract: **"If the signs do not follow, something is wrong with our 'believing.'"** She is not honest enough to indicate by asterisks or otherwise, that the omission has been made. If this is not an example of "handling the word of God deceitfully" (II Cor. 4:2 KJV), then we do not know the meaning of that phrase! It is almost useless to attempt to reason with people who will deliberately handle the Word of God in a manner like this.

It is inexpressibly pitiful how willfully blind people become when they are overtaken by the Tongues Movement. One can neither argue nor reason with them. They have had an "experience," and that "experience" is put ahead of the Word of God, and, of course, of anything else. Oh, a thousand times better it is to doubt your "experience," no matter how sweet it may have seemed, than to doubt the Word of God, which is "forever settled in heaven."

An example of the uselessness of any attempt to reason with the folks in the grip of the Tongues Movement, occurred in this city (Long Beach, California) sometime ago. To make sure that we are not misrepresenting, we were very careful to secure reliable testimony to the truthfulness of what we are about to state. A Pentecostal preacher, defending the Tongues Movement, as many as three times made the statement publicly within his church: **"They tell us that tongues is of the devil. All right, if it is of the devil, we'll go down with the devil"**! The wife of this minister wrote us a letter, informing us that, before preaching against the Tongues Movement, we should be very careful not to become the victim of false reports. We wrote her, requesting her to deny that her husband had made the above statement, or a statement to that effect, and the only answer we have received is absolute silence, all of which goes to show that if these people are deceived in their experience, they prefer to continue so.

# 10. The True Gift Of Tongues Surely Would Be Productive Of "The Fruit Of The Spirit."

The Tongues Movement is lamentably lacking in this fruit.

Nowhere do we read that speaking in tongues is numbered among "the fruit of the Spirit." We do read: **"But the fruit of the Spirit is love, joy, peace, patience, kindness, goodness, faithfulness, gentleness, self-control"** (Gal. 5:22). Now, consider those fruits carefully. No one knowing the victims of the Tongues Movement will accuse them of an undue amount of "meekness"; while "self-control" is a matter which they themselves declare must be thrown to the winds, if the "experience" is to be received.

Note once more the solemn admonition of Paul to the members at Corinth, that when they spoke in tongues, it was to "be decently and in order" (I Cor. 14:40); otherwise, should "outsiders or unbelievers enter, will they not say that you are out of your minds"? (I Cor. 14:23). The Apostle then goes on to declare that when the gift of tongues is exercised, it should bear somewhat of the precious fruit of prophecy; that is, should an unbeliever come in, he will see precious fruit, and, **"so falling down on his face, he will worship God and declare that God is really among you"** (I Cor. 14:25). All our experience touching the modern Tongues Movement has been to the contrary. Believers, as well as unbelievers, who have visited their meetings, have failed to return with the report that "God is really among you." Their reports are usually anything but that. Now, the Lord Himself gives us the right to judge a tree by its fruits: "Thus you will recognize them by their fruits" (Matt. 7:20). Fit words will not permit us fully to describe much of the demonic fruit of this Tongues Movement. Yet, in order that we may appraise the "tree by its fruits," we propose now to give you some of the undeniable fruits that have grown on this tree.

Sir Robert Anderson, in his tract on "Spirit Manifestations and Gift of Tongues," sets forth the following:

> "The career of H. J. Prince, of the Agapemone, deserves a passing notice in this connection. There lies before me as I write, a statement from the pen of his relative, the late Mr. A. A. Rees, of Sunderland, whom I knew personally as a man of sound judgment and a true Christian minister. For five years at Lampeter College, Prince and he were 'bosom friends,' and he adds:
>
> "'Nor did I ever see or hear of an individual more thoroughly devoted to God than he was during that period... His private life, of which I was a perpetual eyewitness, was in harmony with what he appeared to be in public... He was usually blessed, both in the edification of saints and the conversion of sinners, long before he entered the public ministry. He was a man of prayer and self-denial; and few were more deeply acquainted with the Scripture.
>
> "He then goes on to speak of Prince's fall. A book he read about the ministry of the Holy Spirit led him to give himself up unreservedly to the Spirit's guidance. From that time, his desires deepened to do the will of God in all things. As he grew in this habit of yielding absolutely to spiritual guidance, the Bible became

less and less his study, and he ended by neglecting it altogether. Being thus guided in every detail of his daily life, he no longer needed the Written Word; and the total abnegation of his own judgment followed. This complete surrender of mind and will—his entire personality—to what he believed to be the guidance of the Holy Spirit, left him a prey to the terrible delusion in which he was at last engulfed. Oh, the pity of it, the pity of it'! The details of the disaster would gratify none save the prurient and the profane."

Thus that which began sweeter than honey, closed with that which was more bitter than gall!

A tract entitled, "Is the Tongues Movement of God"? by the great evangelist, Dr. R. A. Torrey, contains the following testimony:

"The spirit who manifests himself in the meetings of the Tongues people is anything but the spirit of a sound mind. But the confusion, as dishonoring as it is to the Word of God, and as plainly as it is rebuked by the Word of God, is not the worst thing in the Tongues Movement. There has been, as said above, gross immorality connected with it. The originator in point of time of the modern 'Tongues Movement' was arrested for grossest immorality, a form of immorality for which we have no name in our English language, though it is described in the first chapter of Romans. Another of the most prominent, perhaps the most prominent, leader in the State of

Ohio, was convicted of crime with a young woman, though he himself was a married man. In a number of instances, men and women leaders in the Movement have been proven guilty of the vilest relations with one another. In many instances, the Movement has seethed with immorality of the grossest character. This is not to say, for a moment, that there are no clean-minded and well-meaning men and women in the Movement, but the Movement as a whole has developed more immorality than any other modern movement, except Spiritism, to which it is closely allied in many ways. Two of the leaders of the Movement went from this country to India, and for a while had a following among some of the most prominent Christian workers there, but some of those who went into it were so shocked by the indecencies that developed in connection with it that they came out. In numerous instances, as the 'Tongues Movement' developed, it became evident that it was demoniacal."

The writer could quote other such testimonies from men of highest authority. The recent doings about a certain well known "Temple" in Los Angeles are well known to the public. We quote from "This Is That," an autobiography, being the "Personal Experiences, Sermons and Writings of Aimee Semple McPherson, Evangelist":

"Before the marriage took place, however, I made one stipulation wherein I told my husband that all my heart and soul was really in the work of the Lord and that if, at any time in my life, He should call me to go to Africa or India, or to the Islands of the Sea, no matter where or when, I must obey God first of all. To this he agreed and we were married under those conditions, and settled down in a furnished apartment." (Page 71).

Evidently a sort of **trial marriage!** "Married under those conditions"—conditional marriage, near kin to free-love-ism! **"I must obey God first of all"**—and in doing so, she stood ready to place her emotional impressions, or her revelations through 'tongues,' or bath, above the certain and settled revelation of God: **"For a married woman is bound by law to her husband while he lives, but if her husband dies she is released from the law of marriage. Accordingly, she will be called an adulteress if she lives with another man while her husband is alive. But if her husband dies, she is free from that law, and if she marries another man she is not an adulteress."** (Rom. 7:2-3).

In the light of God's Word, since Mrs. McPherson not only left her husband without cause, but afterward became the wife of David Hutton, what must she be called? Yet, this high priestess of the tongues movement claims a super-holiness wherein she acts ever under a special unction of the Holy Ghost!

Let the Master Himself speak further: **"But I say to you that everyone who divorces his wife, except on the ground of sexual immorality, makes her commit adultery, and whoever marries a divorced woman commits adultery."** (Matt. 5:32).

And did she "put away" her husband **"for the cause of fornication"**? Anything but that! She candidly admits that he pleaded with her to "be happy and act like other folks." She confesses that "a dozen times a day" she would stand before a looking-glass and soliloquize:

> "Now, see here, my lady, this will never do! What right have you to fret and pine like this? Just see those shining, polished floors, covered with soft Axminster and Wilton rugs. Just look at that mahogany parlour furniture and the big brass beds in yonder, the fine bathroom done in blue and white, the steam heat, the soft-shaded electric lights, the pretty baby's crib with its fluff and ribbons, the high-chair and the rocking-horse. Why aren't you glad to have a home like this for the babies, as any other mother would be"? (Page 72).

Then she continues soulfully to relate her experience until the night came in which she decided to turn her back on her husband and "obey God"! She says:

> "Mother now being in Canada, I telegraphed there for money; and when alone in the house one night, phoned for a taxicab, and at eleven o'clock bundled my two babies inside while the chauffeur piled the two suitcases on top, and away we sped to catch the midnight train for home and Mother... God was with me and I was conscious of His leading and support at every step. With my little baby clasped in one arm and Roberta sleeping in the other, I held them tightly to me, as the immensity of what I was doing swept

over me... Setting forth alone—at midnight—almost running away with my two babies—weak in body–empty and lean in my soul no earthly arm to lean upon—no visible open door before me—no living friends—no flowers or 'God bless yous.' **But Oh, I praise Jesus for the experience!**" (Pages 77 and 78).

Imagine praising Jesus for the "experience" of running stealthily away from a loving husband, performing faithfully and generously his marriage vows! Again, she continues the sad story:

"I saw the door, the beacon light of God's dear sunlight—His smile of approval, and I was running toward it... When the train steamed out into the night and sped through the fields and the sleepy towns, we were all on board and the babies sleeping as sweetly as they ever had in their lives, in the snow-white Pullman bed. **I was obeying God.**" (Page 79).

"**I was obeying God**"! Imagine it, if you can, in the light of the clear statement from God's Word: **"To the married I give this charge (not I, but the Lord): the wife should not separate from her husband (but if she does, she should remain unmarried or else be reconciled to her husband), and the husband should not divorce his wife."** (I Cor. 7:10, 11).

People may wonder how this "fundamentalist," whose sermons so often are filled with gospel truth—this woman who makes such high pretensions of holiness—can possibly justify herself in the light of these plain Scriptures. In the light of these Scriptures, she makes no attempt to do so. Hear her own clear statement: **"Paul is the only writer with whom I disagree"**! Too bad for Paul! We cannot help but wonder how she places herself in agreement with Another Who said: "if she divorces her husband and marries another, she commits adultery." (Mark 10:12). The high priestess of modern tongues movements does not hesitate to place her own inspiration above the inspiration of Paul, possibly the greatest of all "the holy men of God" who "spoke from God as they were carried along by the Holy Spirit." (II Pet. 1:21).

Verily, it is no cause for amazement when we learn that the mother of this high priestess of the tongues movement has been twice divorced also—her last divorce one of the cheap and notoriously ill-smelling divorces for sale only in Nevada courts! And, later, the high priestess herself, almost before the honeymooning with David Hutton was over, also divorced him—the cheap-Jack of vaudeville fame, whom she married after deserting a decent husband. Did the same spirit that led her into this last notorious escapade, lead her to "run away" from Mr. McPherson? **We doubt it not!** And, verily, in the sins of the grandmother and the mother "the children's teeth are set on edge" (Jer. 31:29), for the daughter (Roberta) of Mrs. McPherson was in the courts securing a divorce almost before the ink was dry on her marriage license! Does anyone need ask why Angelus Temple is so frequently referred to as "the temple of divorce"—divorce, ruined homes, broken hearts, and suffering children? In the name of all that is holy, we ask: "Are the tongues 'baptisms' within the Los Angeles Temple, baptisms of the Holy Spirit"? If not, from whence do they come?

"We cannot forget our own first experience upon touching the Tongues Movement. In one of the mission churches in the city of Philadelphia, a member of the Tongues Movement from Maine had been invited to preach at a service which was to be followed by Holy Communion. At this Communion, the ordinance of the washing of the saints' feet was to be observed. Of course, the men and the women always sit separately during this service. However, this Tongues preacher insisted that the men and the women mingle in the service; and, with Satan-like cunningness, quoted the Scripture: "In Christ Jesus there is neither male nor female." We presume that he would perform a marriage ceremony in which both the principals. were men, because of the same Scripture! A very close personal friend of ours, Elder Jacob C. Cassell, informed us that he visited their meetings in the State of Maine, where they practiced the salutation of the holy kiss; and, in practicing it, they were very literal in their interpretation of this passage,—for there was, indeed, "neither male nor female"!

In the early days of our ministry in the State of California, in the city where the writer is still pastor, we met a prominent business man for whom we had the very highest personal regard. He seemed to be an intense lover of the Lord, desiring to live as closely to the revealed Word as possible. He had been baptized by the writer. Upon extending him an invitation to unite with the church, he refused, upon the ground. that the writer's church was falling short of a full gospel at one point. Upon inquiry, we learned, to our surprise, that he was seeking "the baptism of the Holy Ghost," which was to be evidenced by speaking in tongues.

He had become a victim of the Tongues Movement! An official of the writer's Church was in his employ. One evening after the doors of this man's place of business were closed, this official remained to finish some work at the desk. Suddenly, the front door was opened, and this business man came in with a Tongues woman. Thinking they were alone, they proceeded with a little "petting party" all of their own, in which they saluted with kisses which could hardly be called "holy." The official of my Church immediately bestirred himself enough to make his presence known. The woman suddenly disappeared from the scene. Then it was that this business man explained that the "love" that was being manifested was "not of the flesh, but of the Spirit"! He also proceeded to defend himself by the Scripture, "In Christ Jesus there is neither male nor female"!

Our next close personal experience with the Movement came when a member of the writer's Church arose in a prayer meeting to testify as to her "wonderful experience," and to declare that she was going to pray that the writer, her pastor, and his Church, should know the "sweetness" of a "baptism" she had come to know. Her testimony came to us as a surprise, for we had not yet learned that she was attending a Tongues meeting in our city. We had always held her and her family in very high regard. We still hold her husband and children in that same regard. To tell the full story of the result of this "baptism" in the life of this woman would be to give, as Sir Robert Anderson says of the case of H. J. Prince,—"the details of a disaster that would gratify none save the prurient and the profane." It is enough if we shall say here that certain "sisters" within the Tongues Movement in our city advised this lady that inasmuch as her husband was not sympathetic with the Tongues brand of religion, their marriage was not "in the Lord." Therefore, they advised her that it would be perfectly proper for her to ignore this marriage and to enter into "a spiritual alliance" with a certain Tongues preacher. This she did! She forsook a fine Christian husband and fine Christian children, and went away with this preacher to conduct Pentecostal meetings over the country. Another wrecked home! Another fine family bowing its head in disgrace and shame! Another bitter fruit of this demoniacal movement! Even while writing these pages, members of three different families came to the writer to testify voluntarily to similar bitter fruits within the inner circle of the families to which they belong. Surely, surely, no gift of the Holy Spirit could bear so continually fruits like unto this!

We have on file a remarkable unsolicited testimony from a man, written to us after he had read the first edition of this booklet. The testimony, you will discover, is most unprejudiced, and therefore of great value. We quote:

> "I have your booklet, Modern Tongues Movement," which shows that you are familiar with this movement in its various manifestations, and it is precisely through my experience and dealings with this movement that certain questions have come up before me for which I would like to find a true and scriptural answer. I have attended Pentecostal meetings ever since the movement started in 1906, but never attempted to take actual part in the work till about one year ago.

"To make a long story short, I was finally brought to a place where I felt it almost a duty to seek the 'Baptism' so-called, for myself. Inside of 48 hours after I started my quest, I fell under the power in a Pentecostal Mission, and went through this very peculiar experience which culminated in my mouth twisting in a strange way and some words coming to me in a foreign tongue. I was exceedingly blessed in my soul and shouted 'Halleluia' till it could be heard a block away. To my surprise, I found that these blessed emotions in my soul seemed to be accompanied with sexual passion in my body. This somewhat astonished me to such an extent, in fact, that I was led to withdraw from the whole thing for a while. I had known of quite a few cases of immorality among Pentecostals, even among preachers. But now comes the final chapter. I am a mission convert and love mission work, or slum work in other words, and the fact is that the Pentecostals at the present time are not only the most enthusiastic mission workers, but the most successful… So, I have almost concluded that I cannot afford to turn down the Pentecostal movement, but the question that I am trying to get light on is this—**why the evil with the good? Why the evil emotions and the blessings coming almost simultaneously"?**

We replied to this letter, giving this brother all the light we could. We now quote from his second letter:

"I desire to thank you very much for your kind and interesting information concerning this peculiar institution. You are certainly at liberty to use my story, though without giving name, any time you want to… I am trying to get as much information as I can from various sources. I have, as a matter of fact, been trying to write a small booklet, giving my experience in detail, but the question before me is really this does the Lord want me to write or publish such a book?… It is this apparent success of the movement that makes me hesitate in publishing anything against them… What I said about the unchaste emotions that followed the 'baptism' is just as I believe I mentioned in my letter. I would have liked to believe that the blessing (for I surely was blessed) came from the Lord and the evil from Satan, but I made some quite careful experimentations at the time, and as far as I could ascertain, the so-called 'power falling' on me (almost as electric shocks) produced both emotions almost at the same time. Psychology can give a partial answer when it says that the spiritual and sexual parts of a man are closely combined and sometimes act in unity, but this would not explain the tongues phenomenon. Much of the tongues are gibberish, but not all. There is certainly an intelligent power back of some of the tongues, that knows not only how to speak various languages, but also knows how to interpret. I would not dare to say either that there may not be a genuine baptism of the spirit."

We have quoted this letter so fully here, because of the apparent absolute honesty and sincerity of the writer—a man with a real desire to know and to do the will of God—a man who has been under the "power," and who seems hesitant to reject it even though he fears it who seems at a loss to make a decision because of the seemingly double source of his "experience." We need to be reminded again and again that demons, even as Satan, may fashion themselves as angels of light (II Cor. 11:13-15)! The testimony, however, coincides with all the rest the sexual emotions are played upon with terrific force, and often with disastrous results, when one goes seeking this unscriptural "experience."

While writing upon this subject, one of the best known and most-loved ministers of Southern California, together with his wife, came to the study of the writer, and told us the story of a very near relative of his, who, caught in this awful delusion, is about to become a case for a psychopathic ward.

As he himself told the story, it appears that this young woman, desiring a manifestation of divine approval in her life, and somewhat attracted by "an elaborate publicity project," began attending the meeting of a certain establishment in Los Angeles where this tongues abomination is considered the final mark of piety. In order to obtain it, she prayed day and night, in her home, at the temple and at the homes of temple devotees, often spending entire nights, where, under the spell of worked-up emotion, the so-called "manifestation of the Spirit" was "prayed down." From such an all-night seance she returned home one morning, walking as in a trance. From this point on, we tell the story exactly as the minister himself consented to write it for us.

"After a demonstration of inarticulate mumblings and hysterical babblings that resembled the jumbled gibberish of a congenital idiot, she announced that she was a chosen instrument of the Lord, that she had been endowed with a special dispensation from heaven with the gift of tongues, and that through divine power she was now able to speak in Hebrew and Sanskrit tongues. Her mother-in-law, knowing the futility of reason or persuasion under such circumstances, decided that the best way to cure the poor girl of her delusions was to urge her to use these gifts, and suggested that they were very opportune, as a Jewish family had recently moved into the neighborhood.

"Fired up by her new-found fancy, she readily made her way to the house of this new neighbor. After being received into the house, she proceeded to tell the good mother in this Jewish home how she was the heaven-inspired agent to reclaim 'the lost sheep of the House of Israel.' She mentioned this gift of tongues as the all-sufficient credential in calling her to this task.

"Then came the demonstration,—jumbled jargon and meaningless mumblings, sputterings, and babblings. For a few moments the Jewish woman looked at her askance. Then, in broken English, which was more forceful than eloquent, shouted above the inarticulate ravings of this poor deluded girl:

"'You shut dat noise up! Das vassen't Hebrew! It issen't even Yiddish! It vassen't eny lanquich at all. You is chust plain nutty! Go back to your own house and don' come back again! God never sent you here! You are chust gone clear what you call it bug-house!' With that, she drove her from the place.

"As this poor woman's husband returned from work that evening, the Jewish woman met him before he reached his home, and implored him to do something to protect the neighbors from his demented wife. This was just a sample of what ensued for several days following. It was not until the Jewish people of the community threatened to have her committed to a psychopathic institution that she desisted from her babblings of this so-called 'Hebrew and Sanskrit.' Being repulsed in all her efforts to convert the Jews by this alleged miraculous gift, she found solace in saying that the time of the Gentiles is not yet up; but, that when God shall decree that Israel shall return unto Him, she will be in readiness for the event. No one will question her sincerity in this matter, but it is easy to see that it borders upon a psychopathic institution."

In "A Warning" against this Movement, published by Dr. A. C. Gaebelein, Editor of "Our Hope," is the following testimony quite apropos to the foregoing testimony. He says: "A godly and reliable brother told us, that in one of these

'Gift of Tongues' Meetings, not very far from New York, a woman arose and 'jibbered' away in strange sounds. A missionary from the south of China happened to be in the service. When that woman gave her utterances, this missionary became very agitated, and then went to the woman and asked her if she knew what language she had spoken. She said she did not know. He told her that she spoke in a Chinese dialect with which he was familiar, but he added, 'It was so vile and obscene—what you said—that I dare not repeat it in English'."

We shall relate here but one more instance. We refer again to the article, "My Experience of Speaking In Tongues," appearing in The Sunday School Times of Feb. 19, 1927. We refer to this article inasmuch as the principals were all members of my own Church. This woman's husband was opposed to the Tongues Movement. She says:

> "Here lay our battle ground, for my opposition to his position was the wedge with which the Evil One tried to wreck our home. Toward the end of the year, it brought my husband from France in great distress of mind over home conditions. He remained home six weeks, using every means in his power to induce me to come out of that deceitful snare. Although promising him I would leave it, I was not yet ready. I had no real desire nor power to break away, so continued on in it while he returned to France to resume his service. I had no real peace of mind or heart, but was filled with fear on the one hand and pride on the other. ... In the deception and pride of my own heart, I deemed myself to be superior in

spiritual matters,—that to me was committed a secret of the Lord, the 'oracles of God,' because I could speak in tongues, and I was led to believe myself a martyr, persecuted by my own husband, for what I called righteousness sake. When he returned home to stay, this atmosphere existed to such an extent that it meant to my perverted thought, either insanity or separation from him and a break-up of the home,—the very thing the enemy sought to produce....

As time went on, I would go away from home to Pentecostal gatherings to be, as I thought, spiritually fed. But at such times I had no hesitation in talking to my friends about home affairs, especially the opposition and so-called persecution of my husband. These friends gave me, mistakenly, a kind of spiritual flattery and sentimental sympathy which went far to strengthen my heart against the man whom the Lord had led me to marry in answer to prayer...

The deeper I went into the experience of speaking in tongues and the movement itself, the farther I got away from my natural and spiritual protector and the nearer our home came to being smashed. Several homes have come under my observation where the break-up has actually occurred, the cause being due to this so-called religious experience, leading in every instance to unscriptural marriage relationship. Thank God, my husband laid hold of God for me, and was the means in His hand of delivering me, and with that deliverance the home was held intact."

**Surely, it is a master stroke of Satan that enables him to "deceive if it were possible the very elect" by imitating one of the gifts of the Holy Ghost exercised in the apostolic church, to wreck the most sacred institution which God ever built- the home and the marriage altar within it!**

The victims of the Tongues Movement seem to be very fond of quoting the passage in Luke 11:11-13. We read:

**"What father among you, if his son asks for a fish, will instead of a fish give him a serpent; or if he asks for an egg, will give him a scorpion? If you then, who are evil, know how to give good gifts to your children, how much more will the heavenly Father give the Holy Spirit to those who ask Him!"**

The trouble in the Tongues Movement is that they ask not for the Holy Spirit, but they ask for a sign. They seek "a baptism,"—"an experience." There is a vast difference between asking the heavenly Father for bread or for the Holy Spirit, and asking Him for an "experience" which He has not promised, and which may be wholly outside the divine will. When a saint steps out of the revealed will of God, and insists on asking for "bread" which is not bread, or for "a fish" which is not a fish, or for "an egg" which is not an egg, he is very apt to receive "a stone," or "a serpent," or even "a scorpion." There is a mass of evidence that the victims of the Tongues Movement have been getting just that,—"stones," "serpents" and "scorpions"!

Since beginning this writing, we have received through the mail a very solemn warning,—"Forbid not to speak with tongues"! The warning, being Apostolic and Biblical (I Cor. 14:39) is well taken. God forbid that we should ever speak a word against any work of the Holy Ghost. Rather die than that! We are not warning against any work of the Holy Ghost. We solemnly warn, however, against the work of the awful powers of hell, which in most cunning subtlety, would impersonate the Holy Ghost, and would deceive the saints of God. We solemnly affirm that any speaking in tongues that ignores the directions of the Holy Ghost Himself, is not of God, but is of the demon powers of hell.

If ever the Holy Ghost again imparts this gift to men, then let us open our hearts to receive it. The writer will be the first to welcome it when it comes with the Scriptural ear-marks of the Holy Ghost, fully tested by the sure and unchangeable Word of God.

## "TEST THE SPIRITS"

We shall let that great "disciple whom Jesus loved, himself inspired of the Holy Ghost, utter the final word of warning and advice:

> **"Beloved, do not believe every spirit, but test the spirits to see whether they are from God, for many false prophets have gone out into the world. By this you know the Spirit of God: every spirit that confesses that Jesus Christ has come in the flesh is from God, and every spirit that does not confess Jesus is not from God" (1 John 4:1-3).**

"TEST THE SPIRITS WHETHER THEY ARE OF GOD." What wholesome advice! In the light of that warning, can any true child of God accept even a "sweet experience" as coming from the Holy Spirit without testing the spirit (or the Spirit) that is back of it? Not to do so, proves that one is unfitted for the gift.

"TEST THE SPIRITS" first of all by the strict tests that God has given us to use to this end in the 14th Chapter of 1 Corinthians. Of these tests we have fully spoken.

"TEST THE SPIRITS" by challenging any spirit that speaks in an "unknown tongue" to instantly confess that "Jesus Christ is come in the flesh." Be careful to distinguish between the confession of the person through whom the spirit may be talking and the confession of the spirit itself. The man may be ready with the confession; but, demand that the spirit speaking shall so confess. Tongues people usually refuse to put this test to the speaking spirit, saying, "We cannot do so, because it would be false and ridiculous to do so." Or, "It would insult the Holy Ghost were we to infer the possibility that He might be a demon." Exactly! Accepting the spirit untested, they refuse to put the test that God has authorized.

Moreover, should one be bold enough to challenge the spirit that is speaking, demanding that it shall "confess that Jesus Christ is come in the flesh," still he will have to be on his guard against deception by the most cunning of evil powers. The Christian Herald told of a "confession" from one gifted in tongues in Sunderland (Eng.). Here it is:

"I felt I must know from God Himself whether what I had received was of God or not. I got on my knees before Him, and questioned the spirit within me: 'Do you confess that

Jesus Christ is come in the flesh?' Immediately my soul was filled with the glory of God, and the Lamb was adored by me as never before. I had never fully really known how to worship before, but the Holy Spirit in me adored Jesus; and that evening I spoke in four or five different tongues."

Do you see the subtlety of this experience? Did the spirit make the confession? No! With all the adroitness of the Prince of Demons, the test was eluded, and an **emotion**—a "sweet experience"— was substituted! It **seemed** good. And it would take a discerning mind, with wisdom from the Spirit of God, to detect quickly the deception. In your very testing, watch for the deception!

Consider, here we close, the experience of Paul and Silas. See Acts 16:16-22. The evil spirit here appears as a genuinely orthodox Fundamentalist! Loudly it endorsed all Paul and Silas taught. Demons prefer to creep in, when possible, where God's true children congregate. Seldom are they Modernists. They know the difference between good wool and cheap shoddy! But what a warning! Was this confession the confession of the poor, demon-possessed woman, or was it really the confession of the demon spirit within her? Doubtless, it was the woman's own confession. In the light of this experience, how it behooves every child of God, into whose temple any spirit seeks an entrance, to apply every God-given test of the Scriptures; and, if it fails in that test **at a single point**, instantly close every door and window!

Finally, may God, by His own Holy Spirit, guide every child of His, keeping your feet from the pitfalls of the most cunning trapper of souls in the universe. It is the fearful ignorance of the subtle wiles of the Prince of Demons that is proving, through Spirtism and demon tongues movements, to be the terrible spiritual downfall of so many souls in these days. May God bless this little booklet as it goes forth on its mission to help dispel that ignorance!

# About The Author

Louis S. Bauman Louis Sylvester Bauman was a pastor, missionary advocate, Bible conference speaker, and author. Born on November 13, 1875, he passed away on November 8, 1950. The son of a traveling minister and evangelist, he dedicated his life to ministry at a young age, inspired by his mother's heartfelt commitment of him to God shortly after his birth.

Dr. Bauman served in various pastorates, including in Philadelphia, Pennsylvania; Mexico; Roann, Indiana; Long Beach, California; and Washington, D.C. His 34-year ministry in Long Beach was particularly influential, growing the congregation to over 1,900 members and inspiring more than 150 individuals to enter full-time Christian service. He also played a key role in establishing numerous new churches across Southern California, leaving a significant legacy through his leadership and evangelistic work.

His passion for the Bible drove him to an extensive teaching and speaking ministry, influenced by renowned Bible teachers like I. M. Haldeman, C. I. Scofield, and A. C. Dixon. He became a leading authority on Biblical prophecy, frequently lecturing at Bible colleges and seminaries such as BIOLA, Moody, Bob Jones University, Multnomah, and Grace Theological Seminary, where he was a founding figure.

Dr. Bauman was also a gifted writer, contributing articles to respected Christian publications, including Sunday School Times, King's Business, and Moody Monthly. He authored numerous works, with his most notable titles including The

Faith, Light from Bible Prophecy, Russian Events in the Light of Bible Prophecy, The Time of Jacob's Trouble, Philemon: An Exposition, The Modern Tongues Movement, and The Approaching End of this Age.

Printed in Great Britain
by Amazon